I0467793

Advance Pattern Coloring

Cloud Aswegan

Copyright © 2012 Cloud Aswegan

All rights reserved.
ISBN: 1522767185
ISBN: 978-1522767183

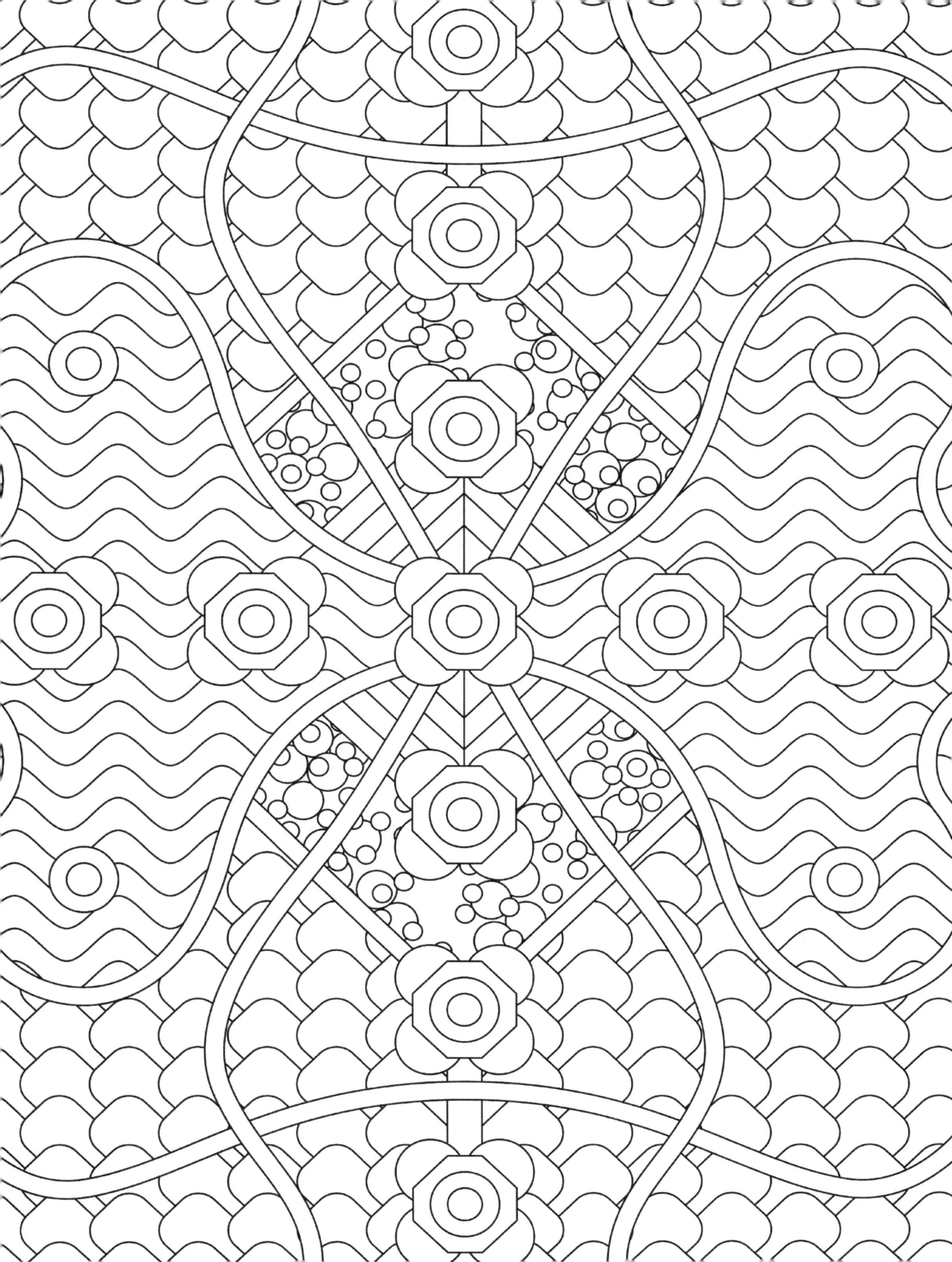

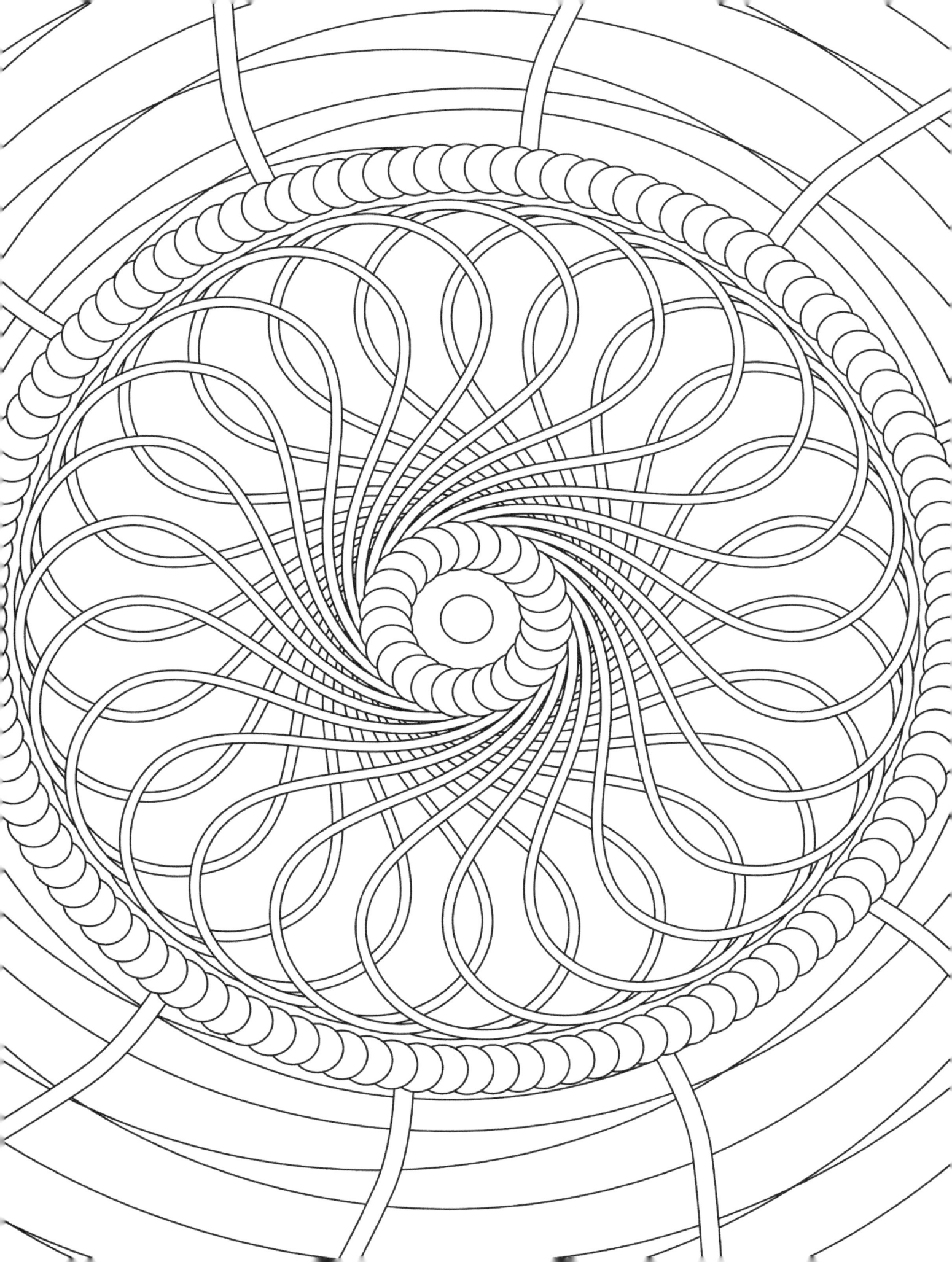

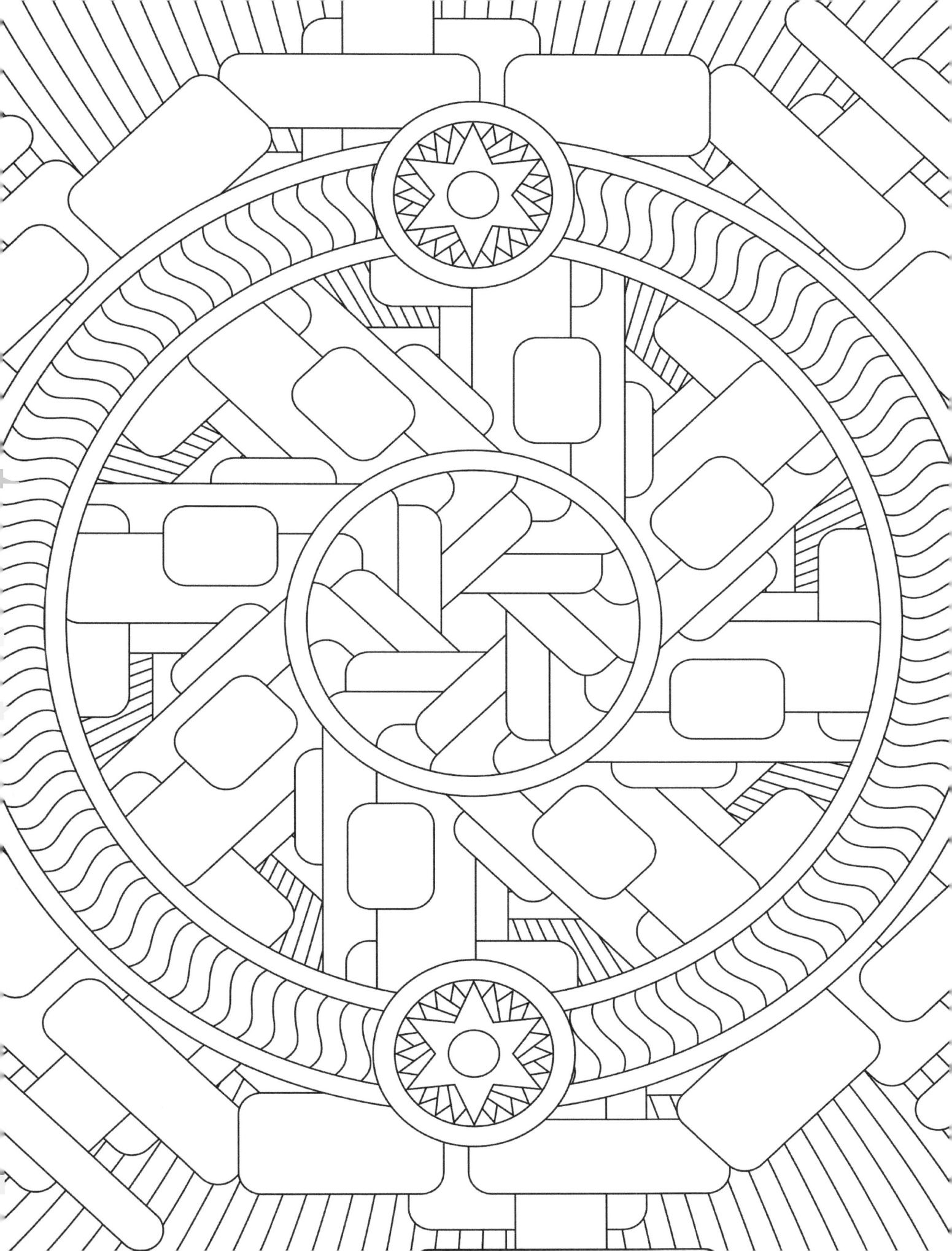

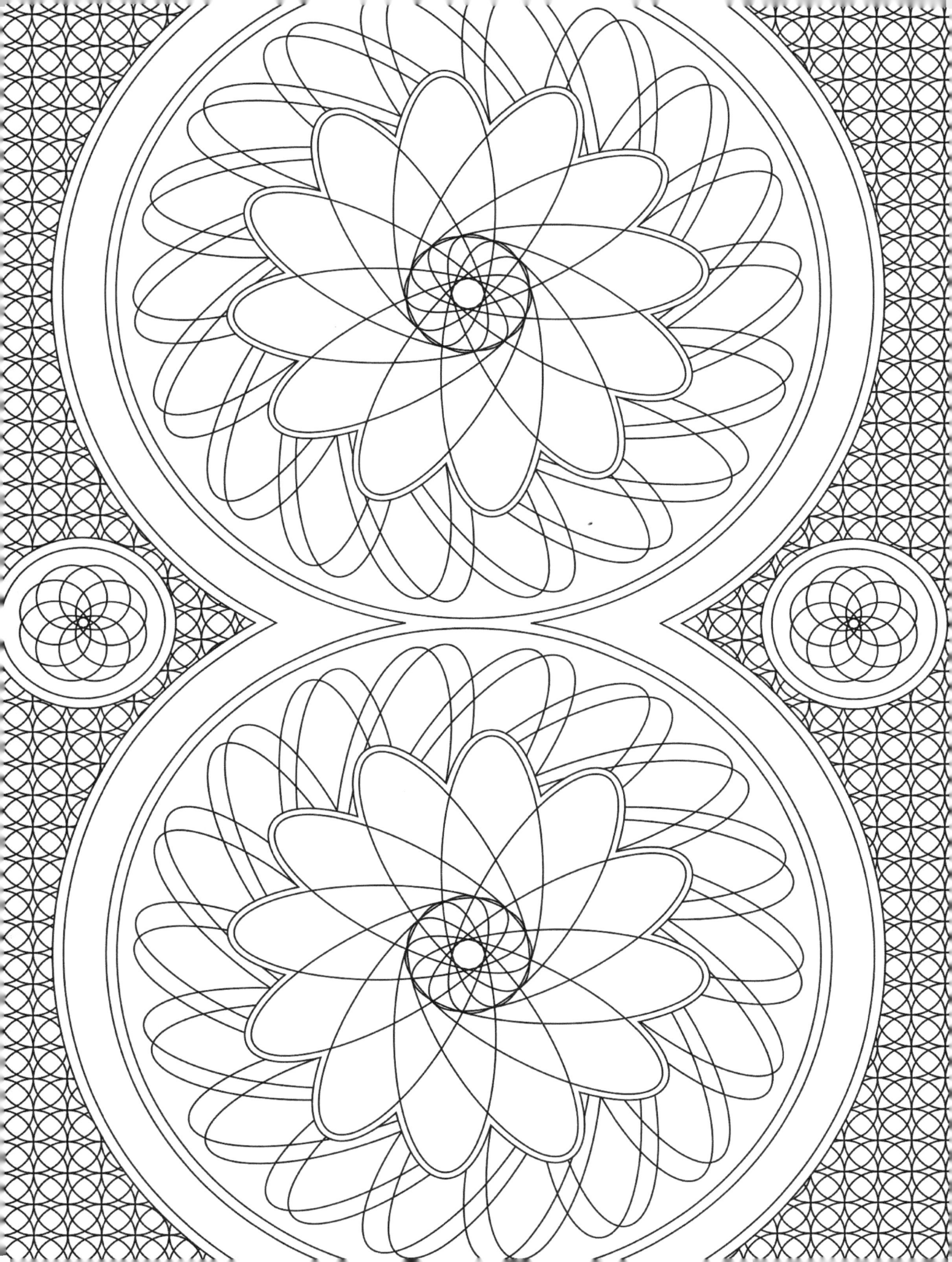

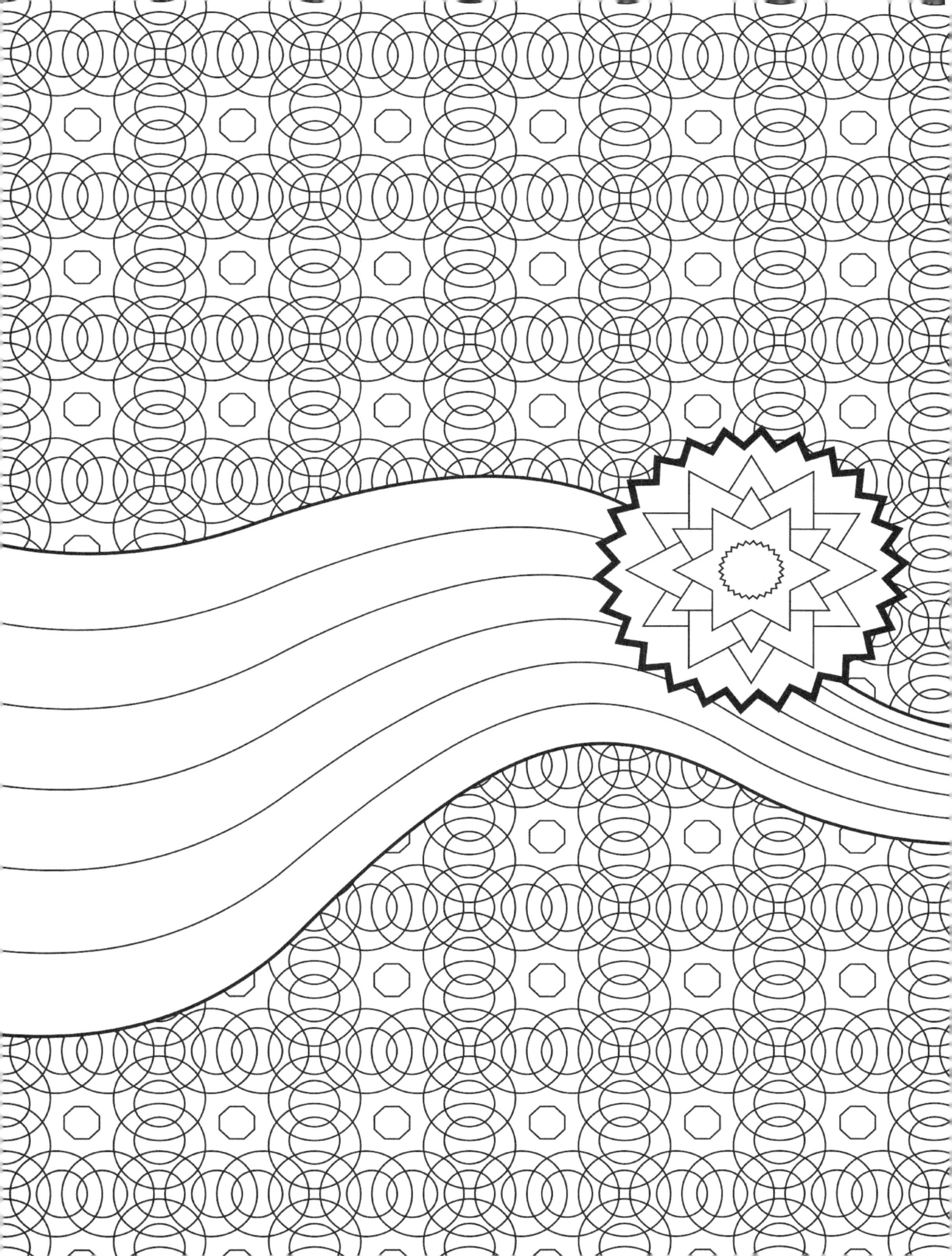

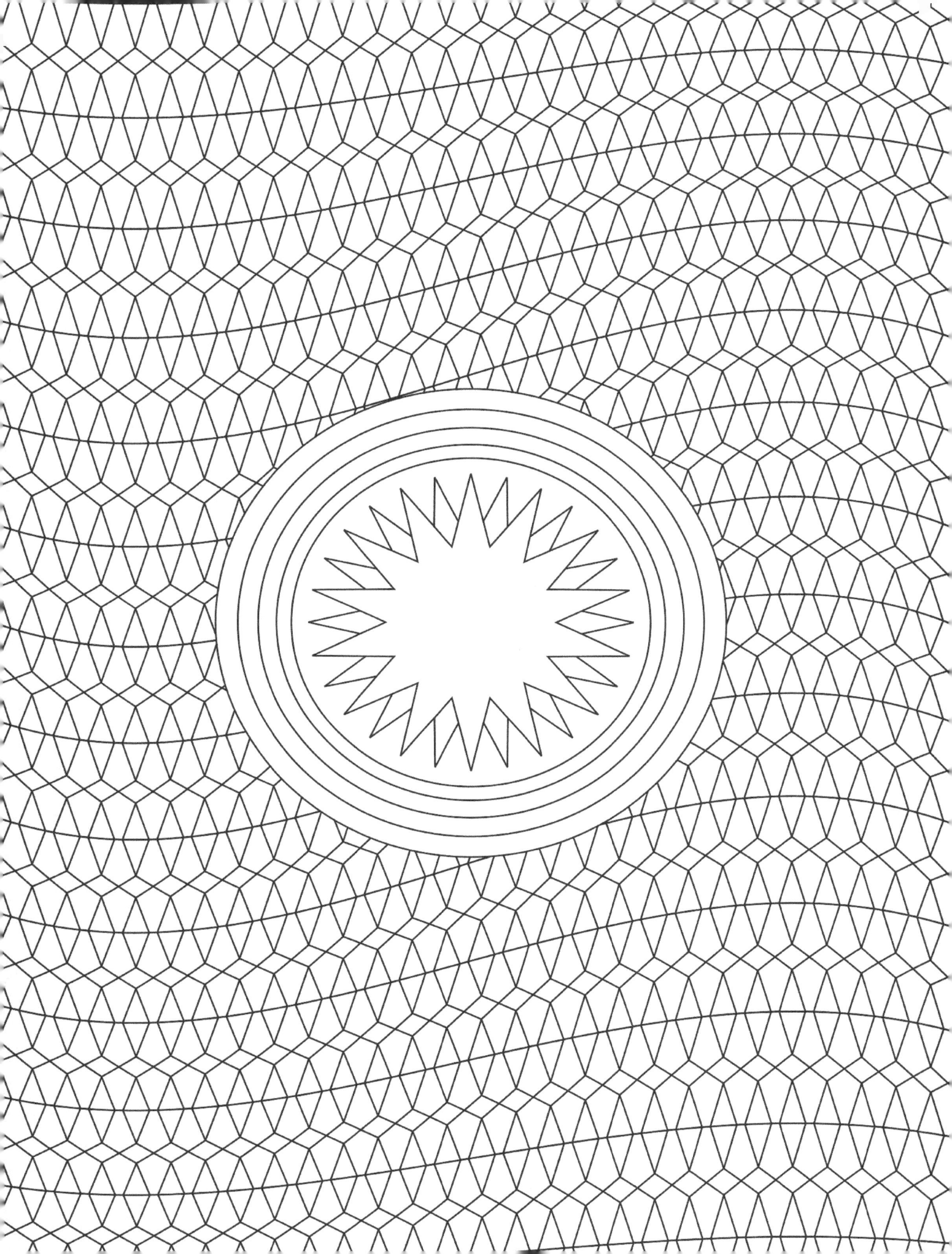

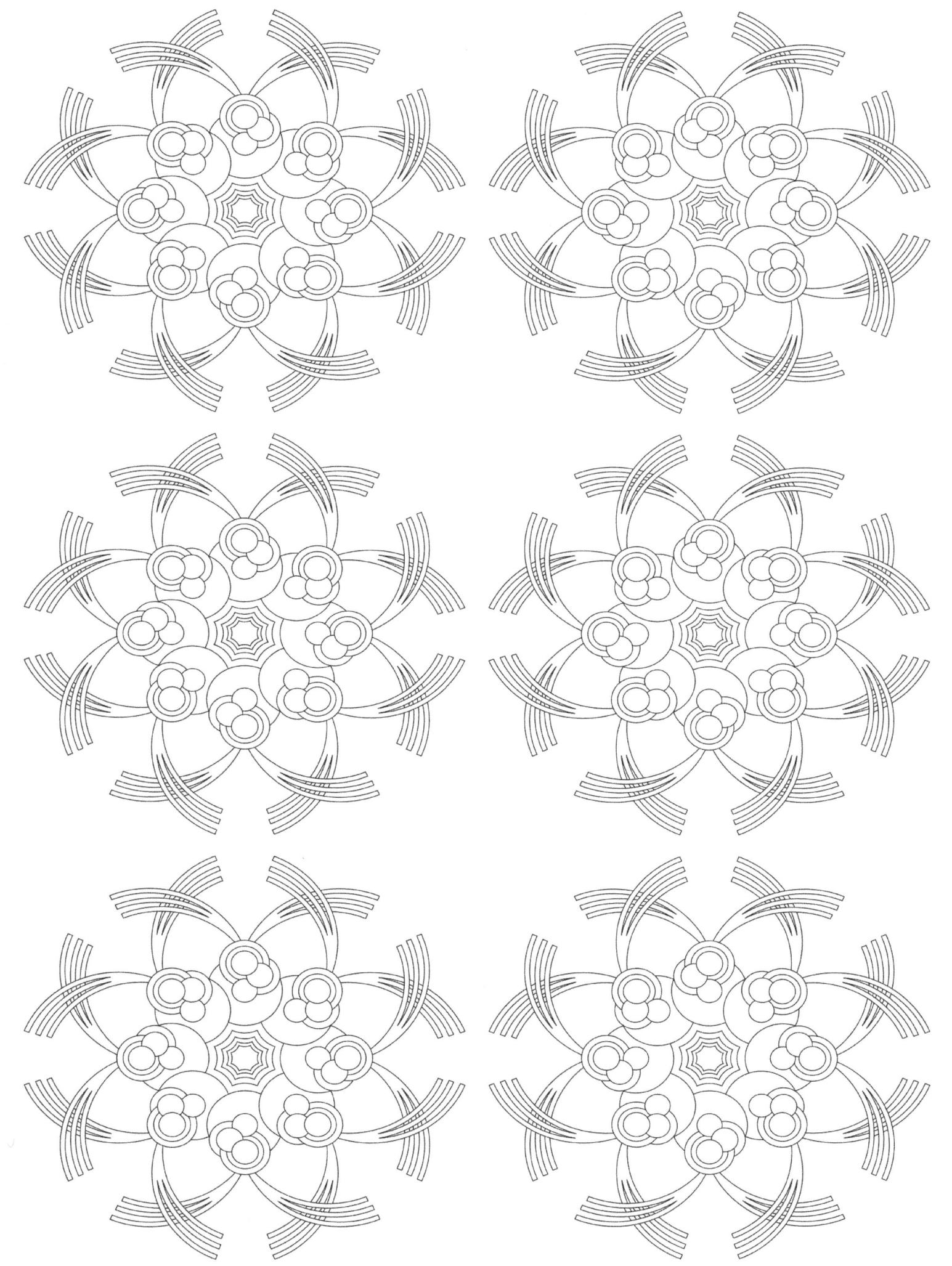

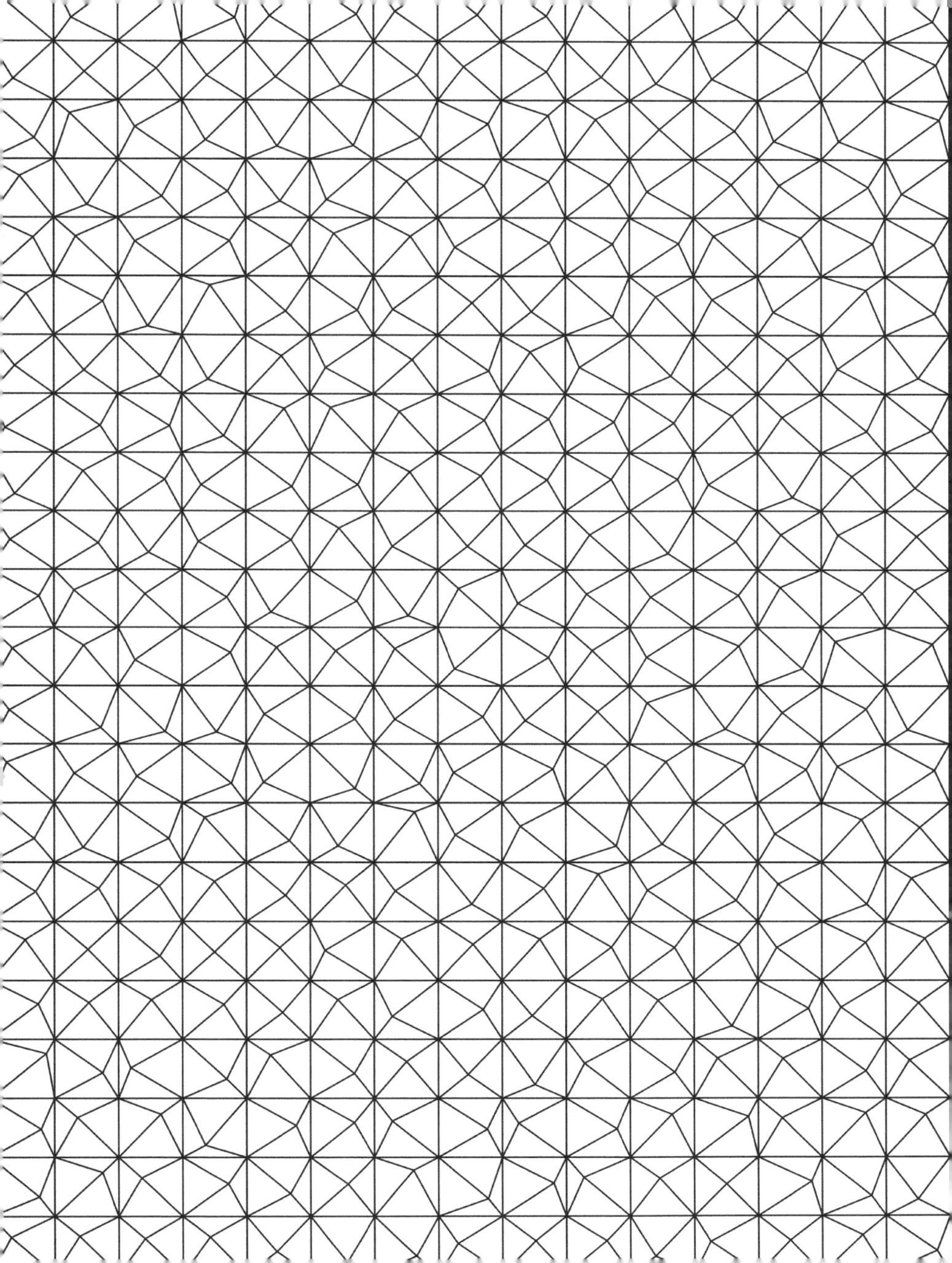

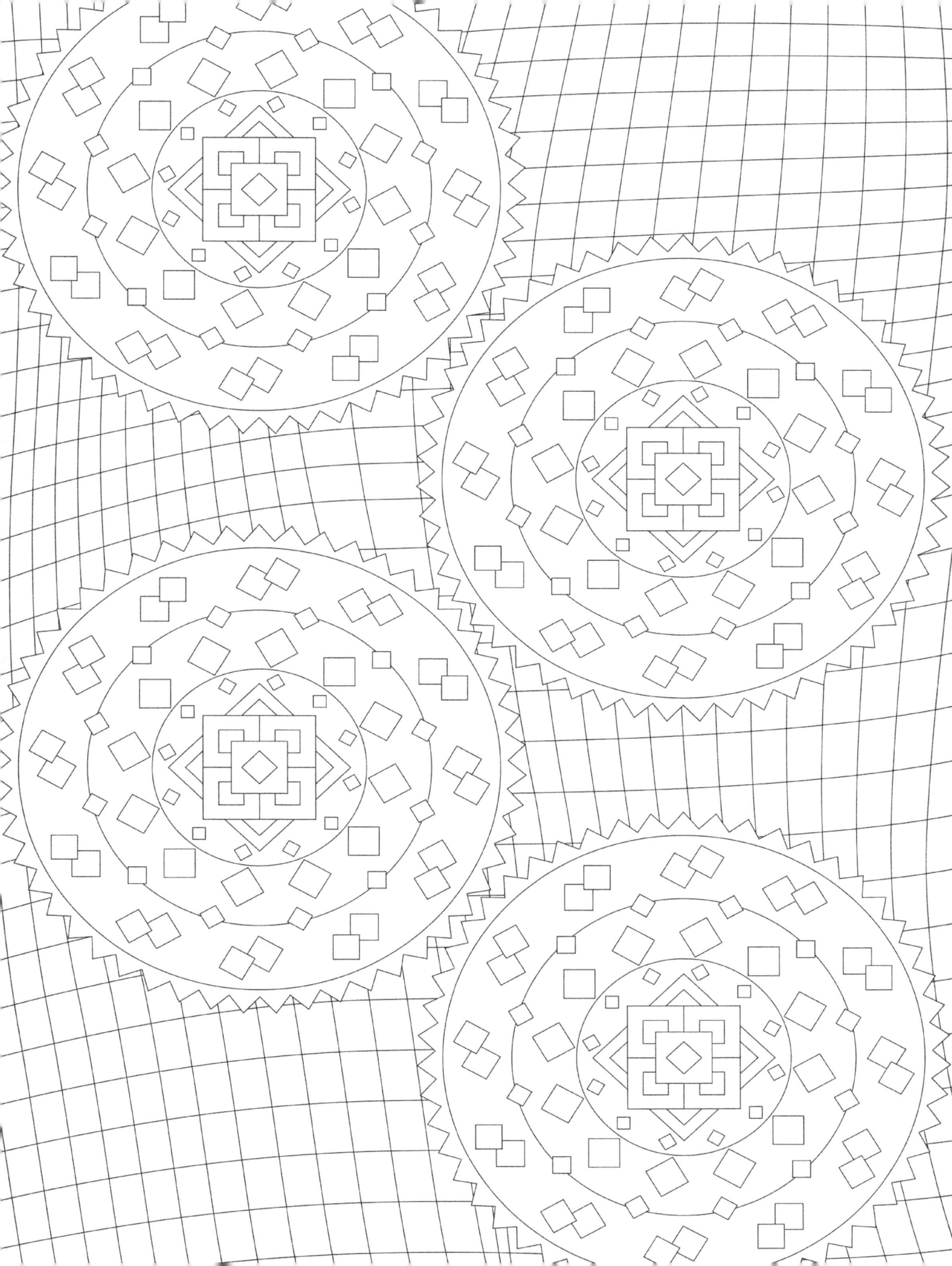

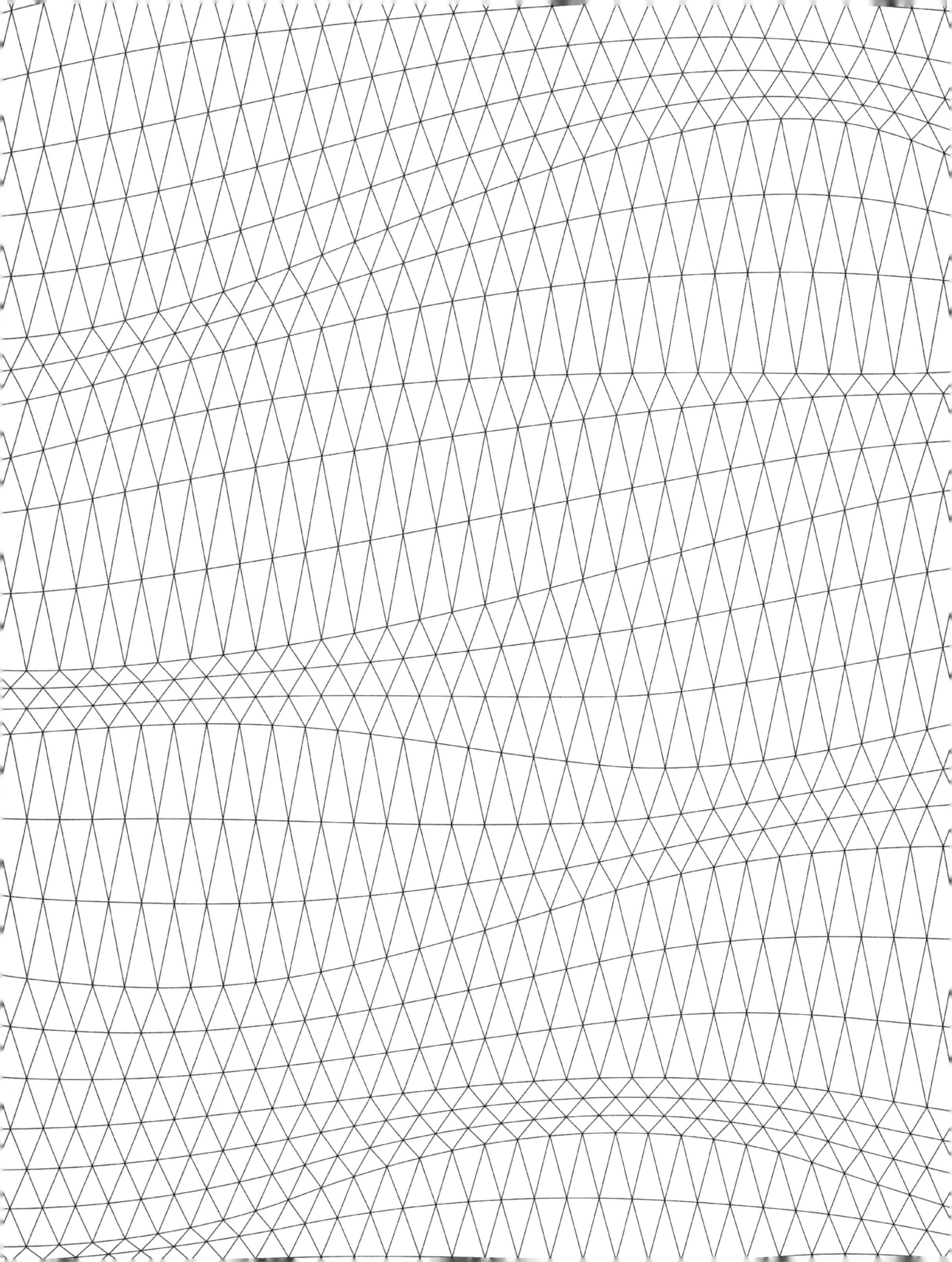

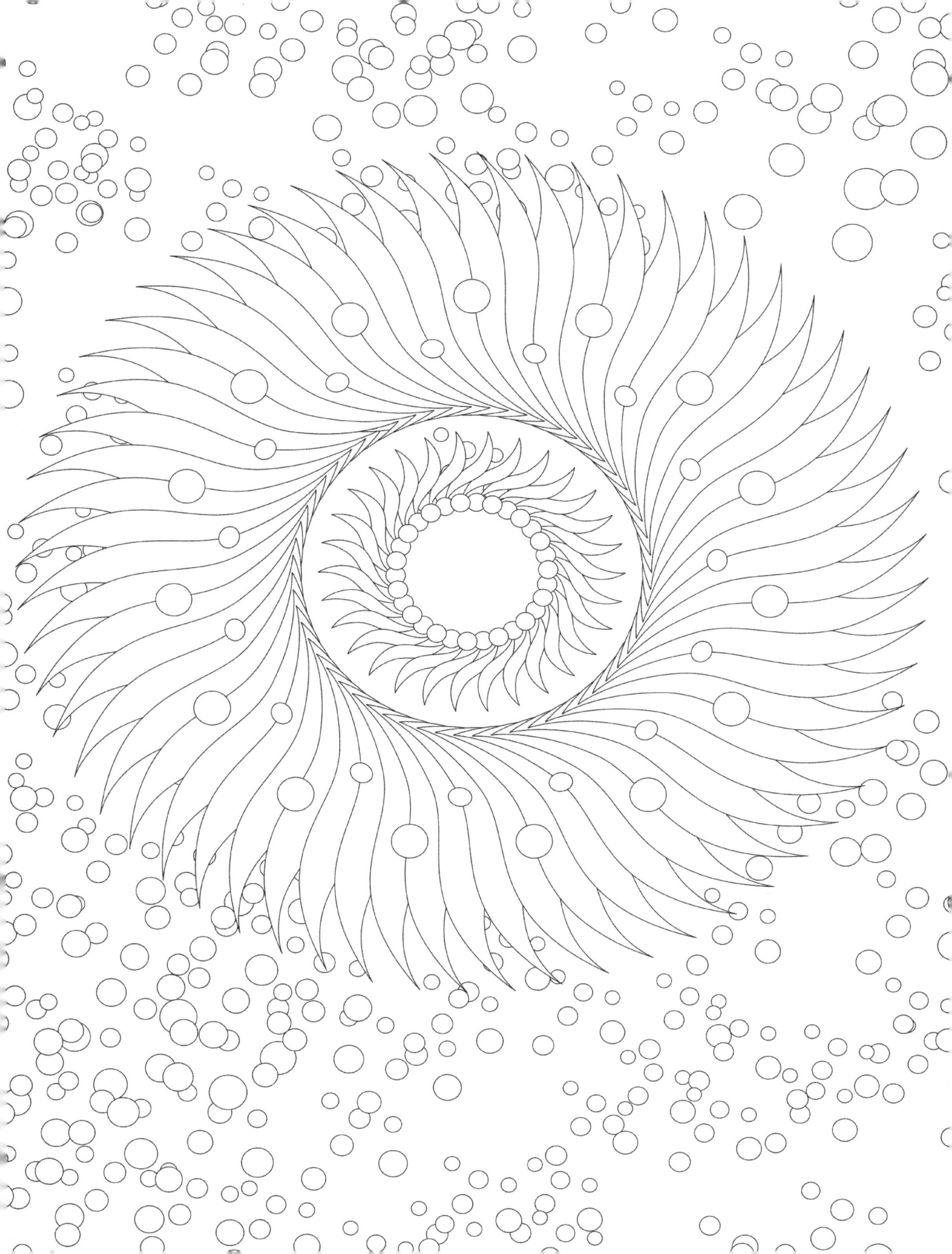

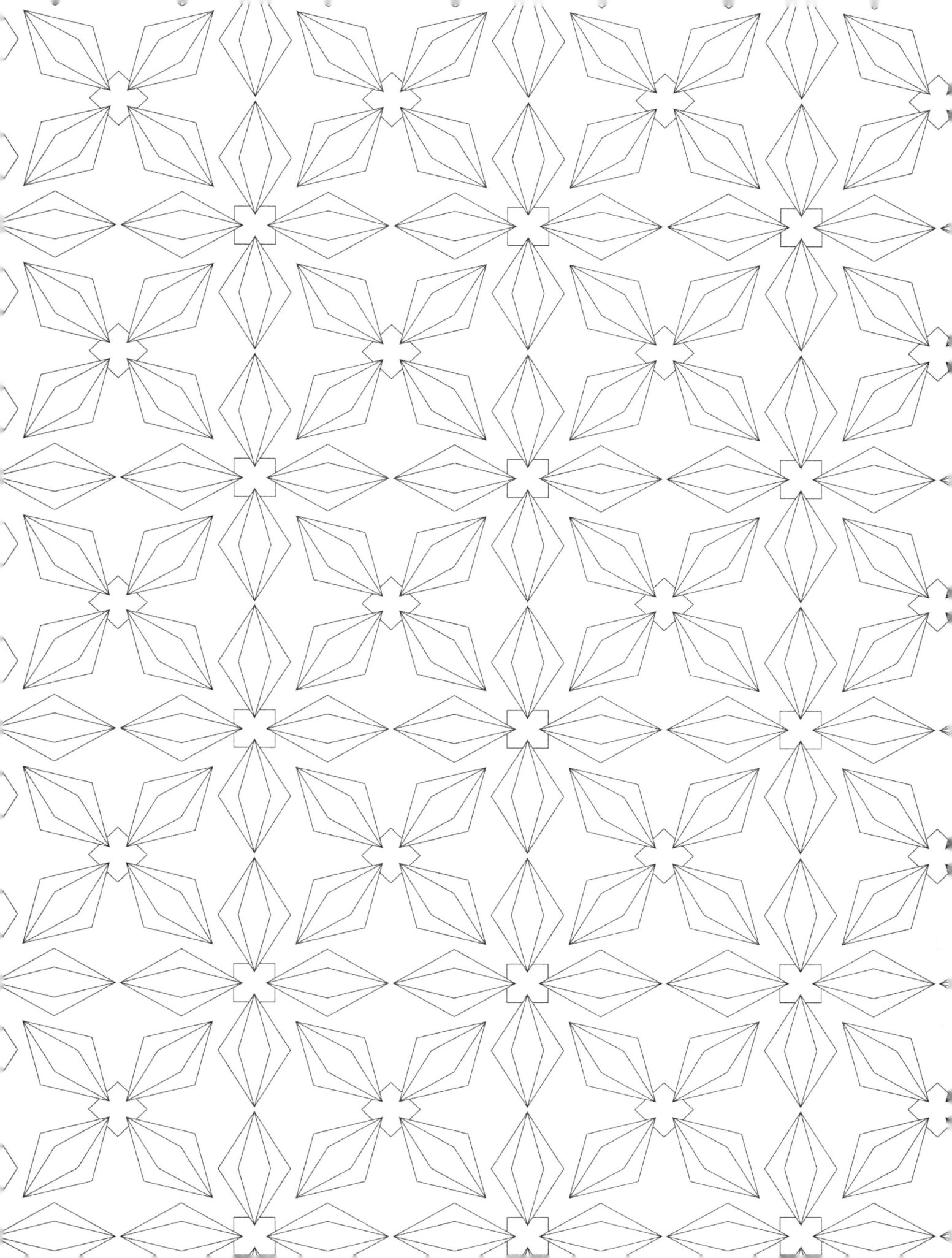

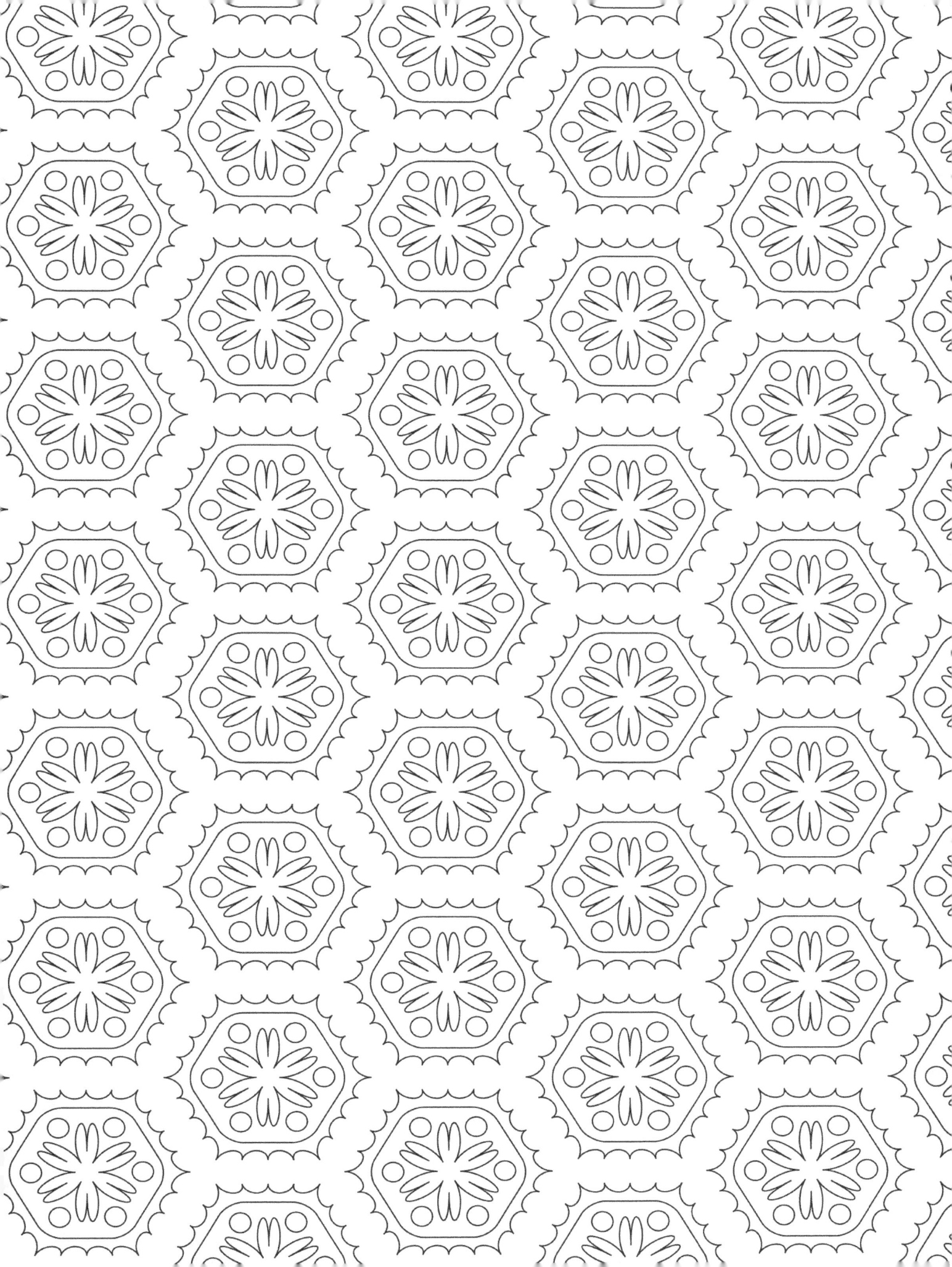

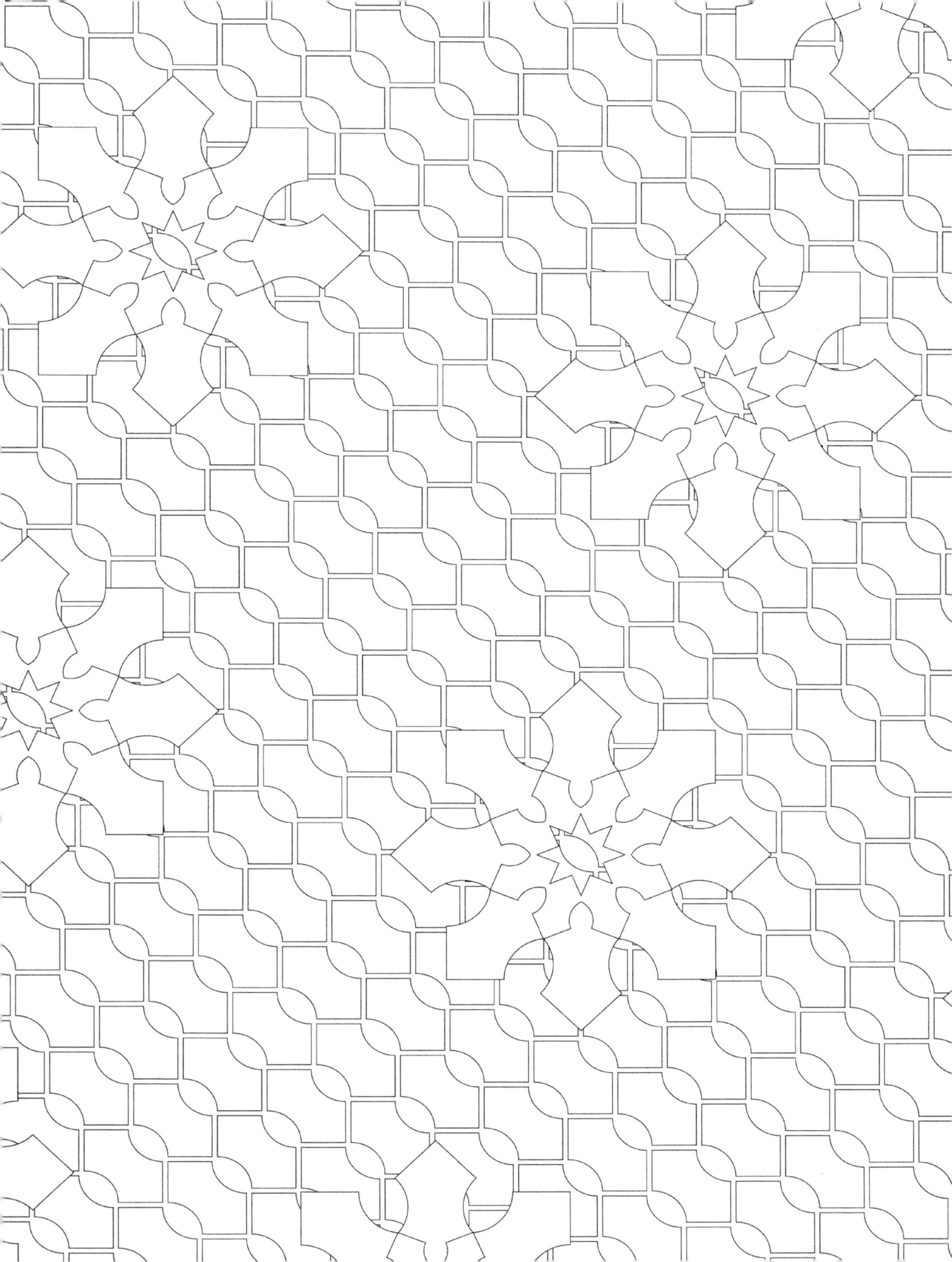

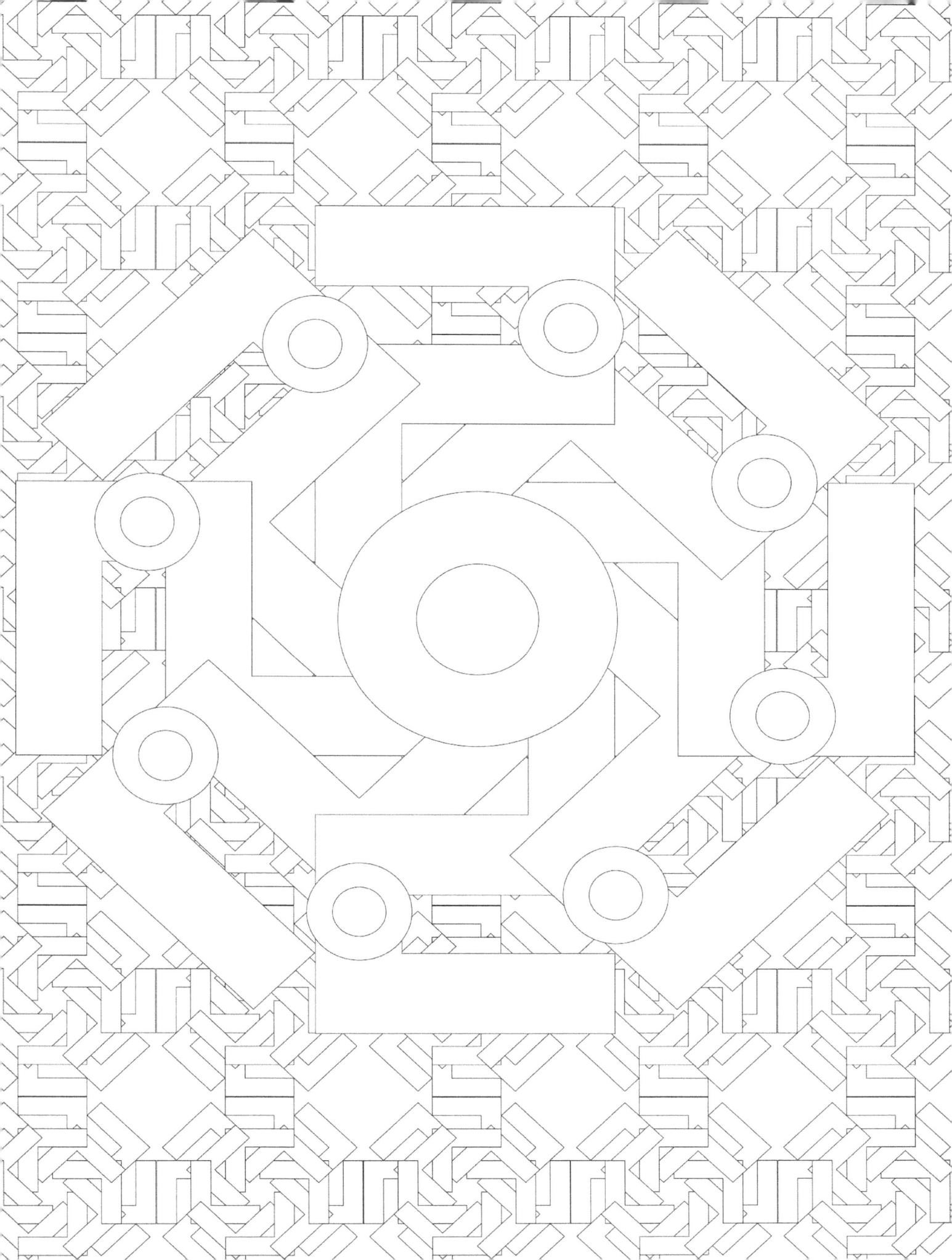

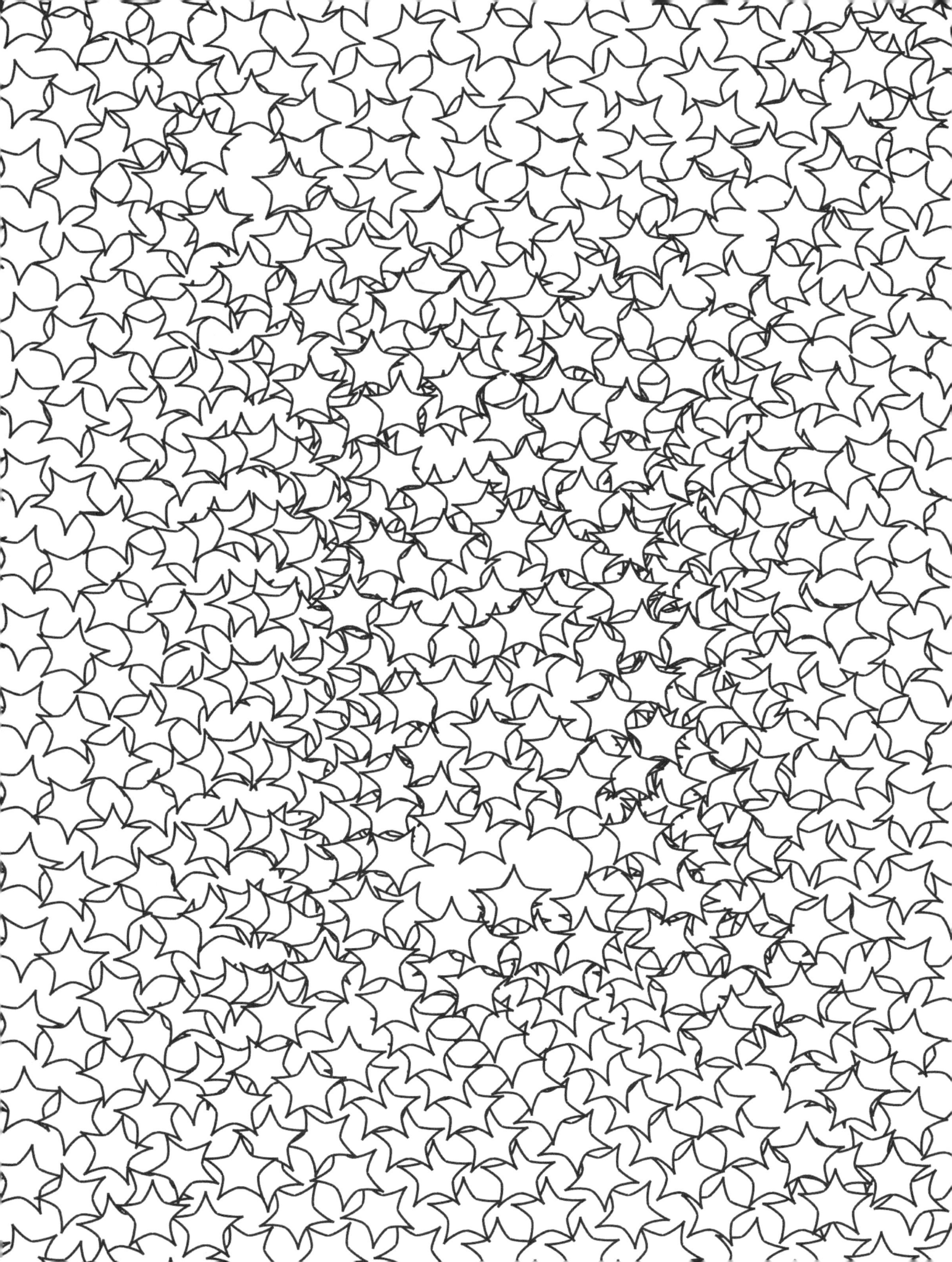

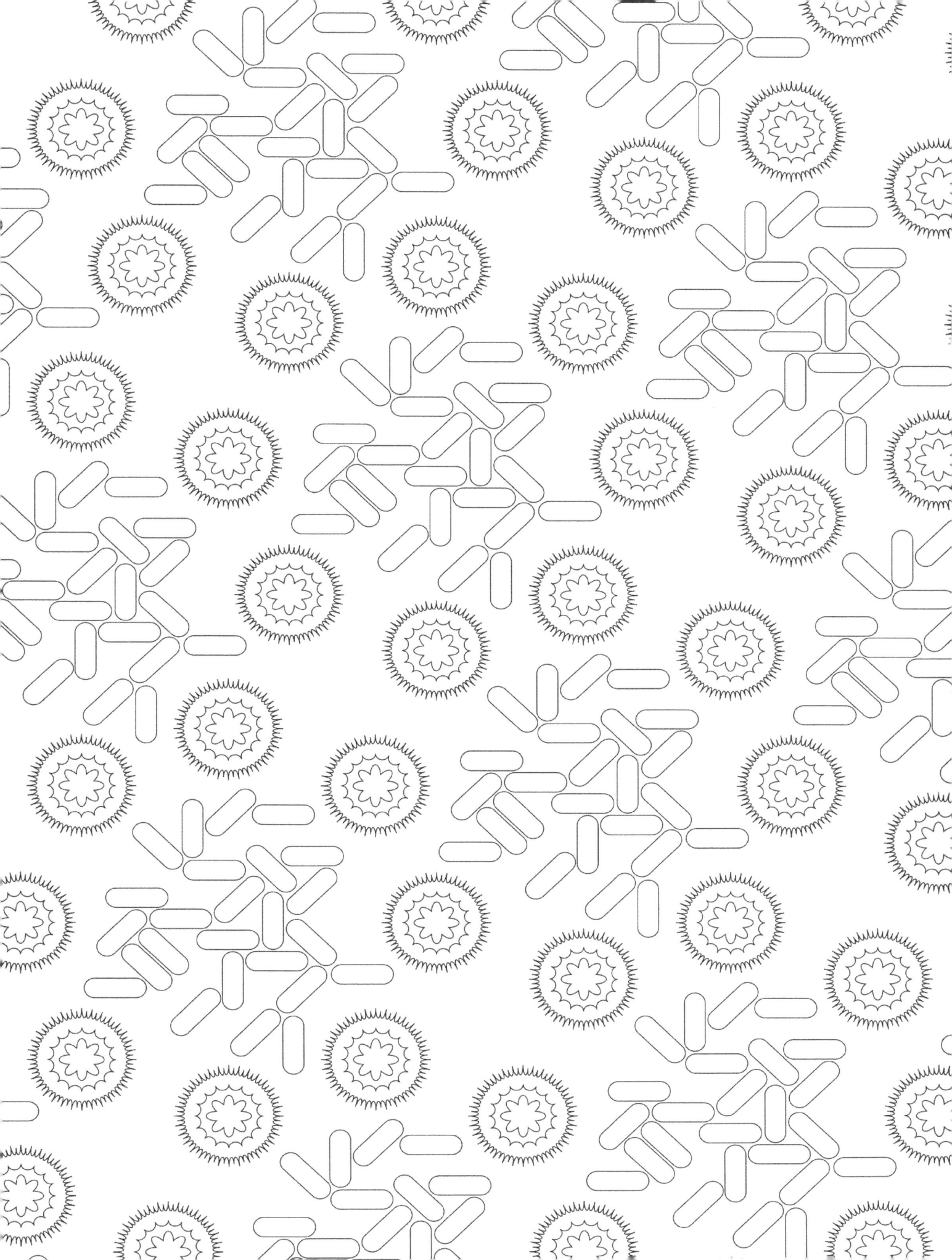

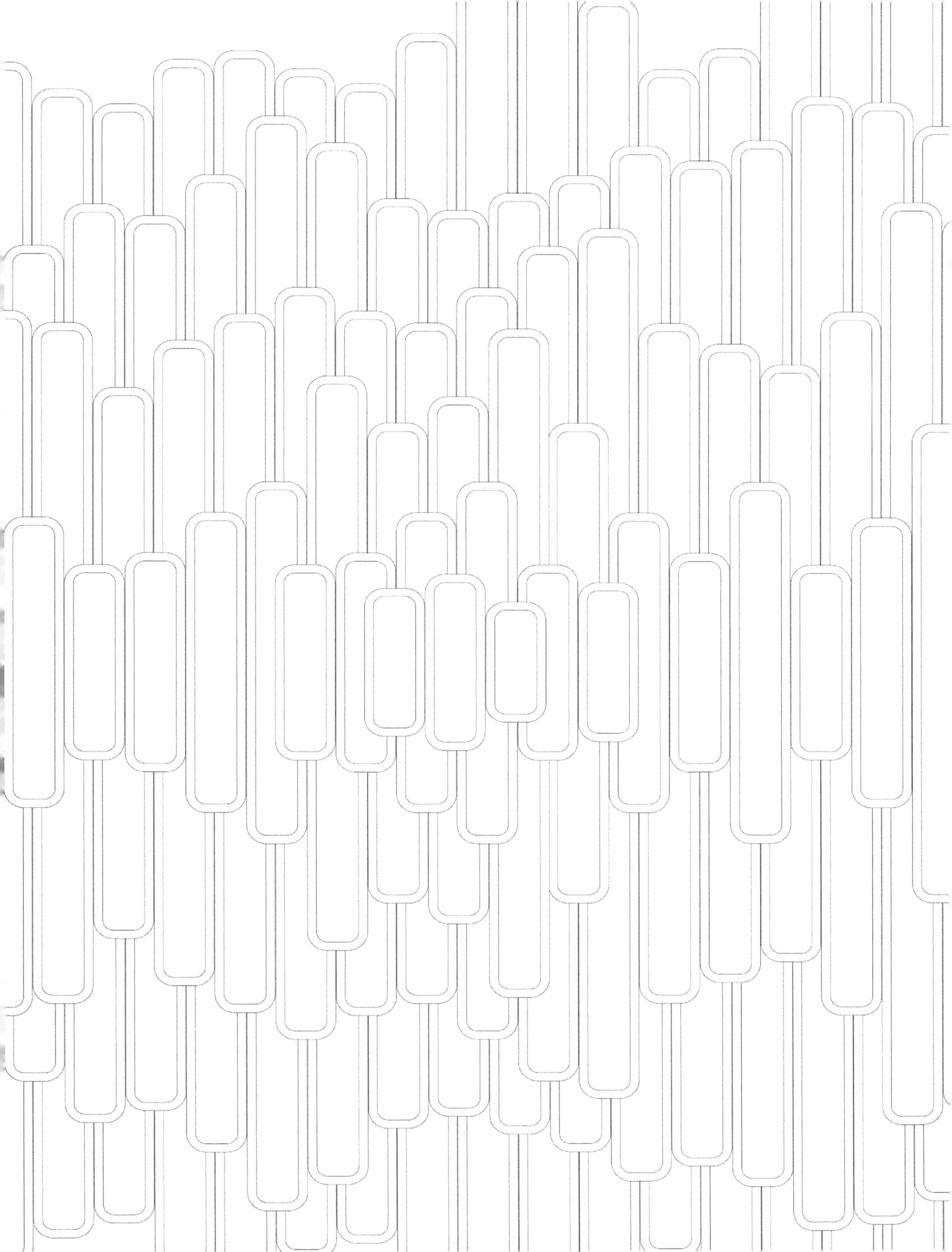

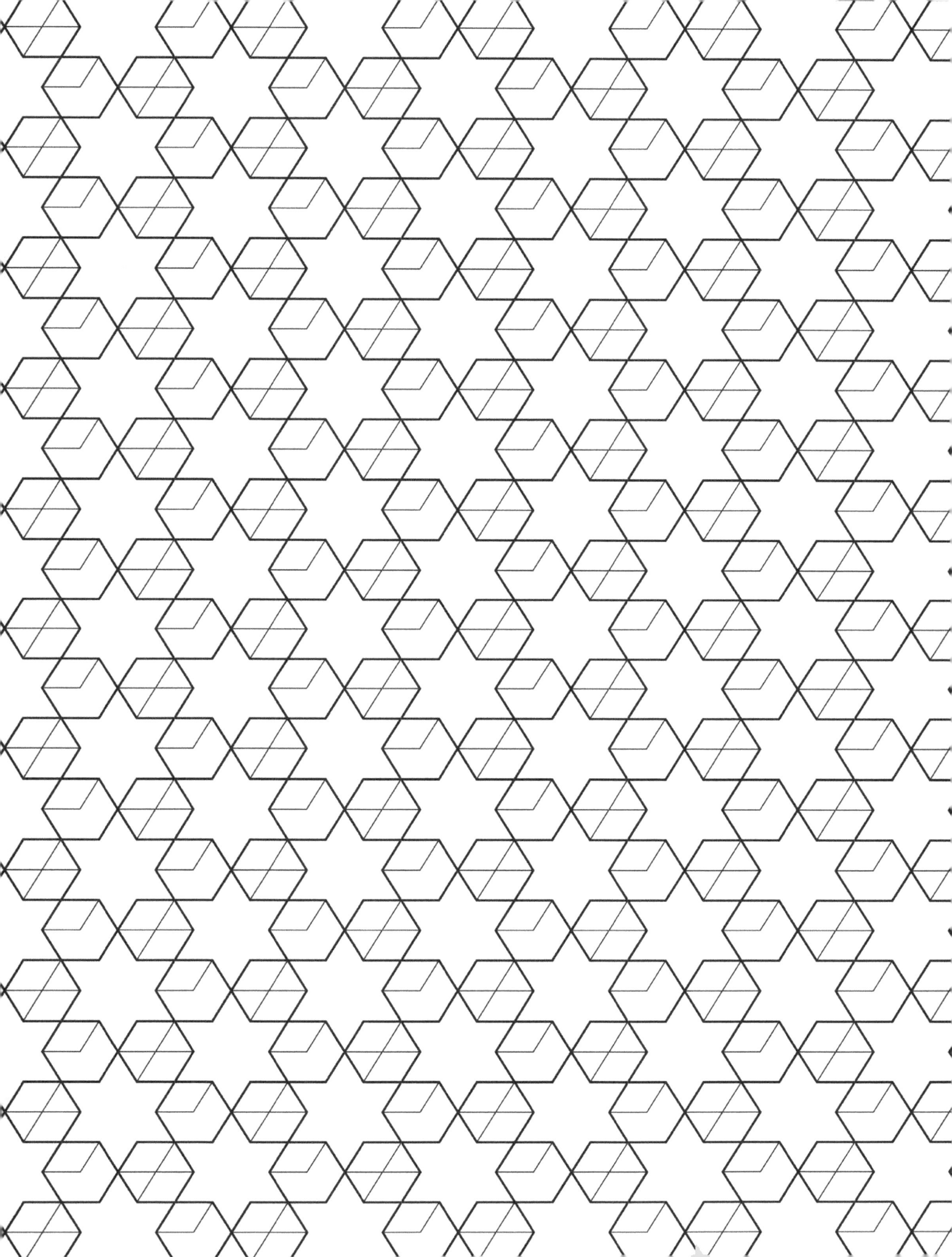

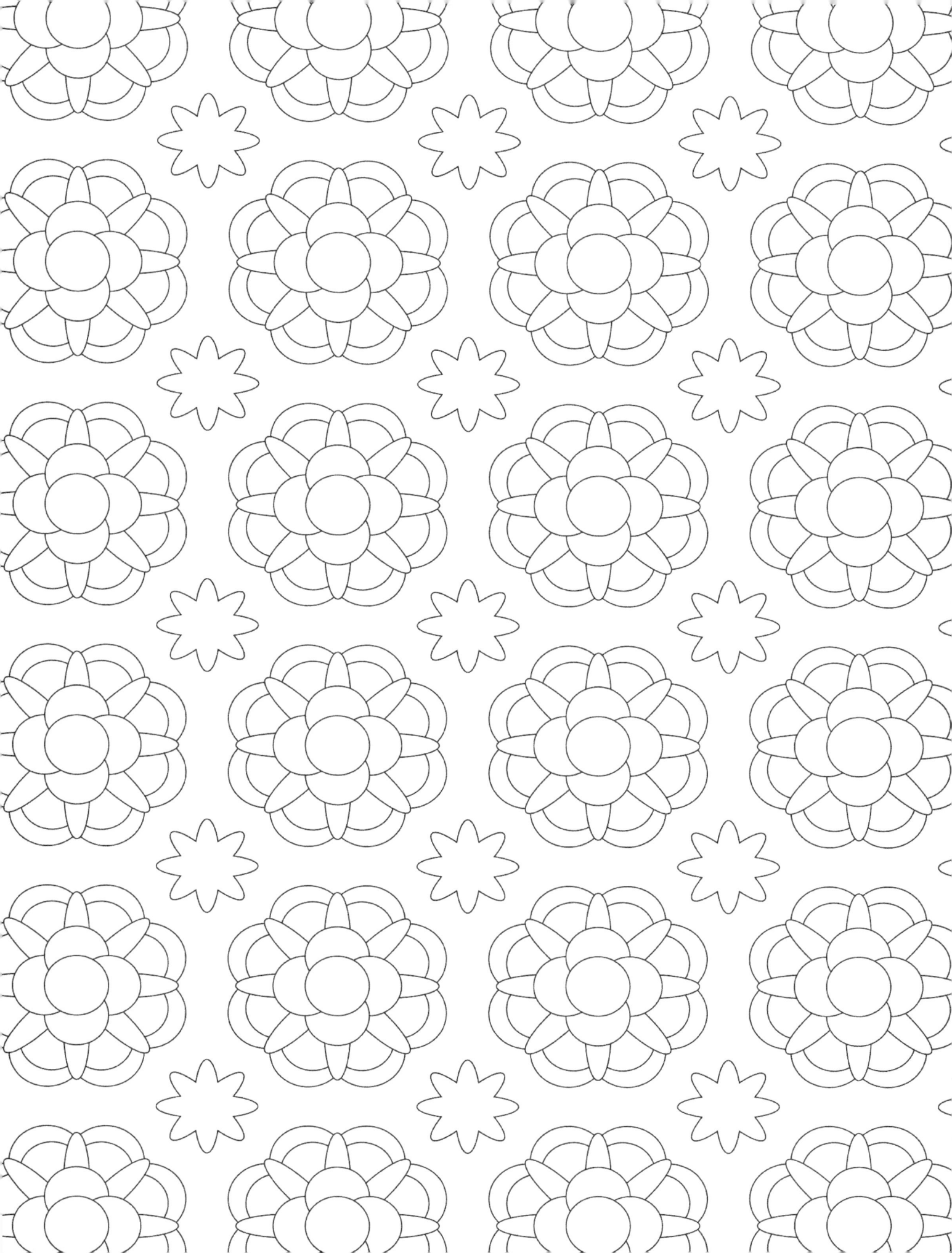

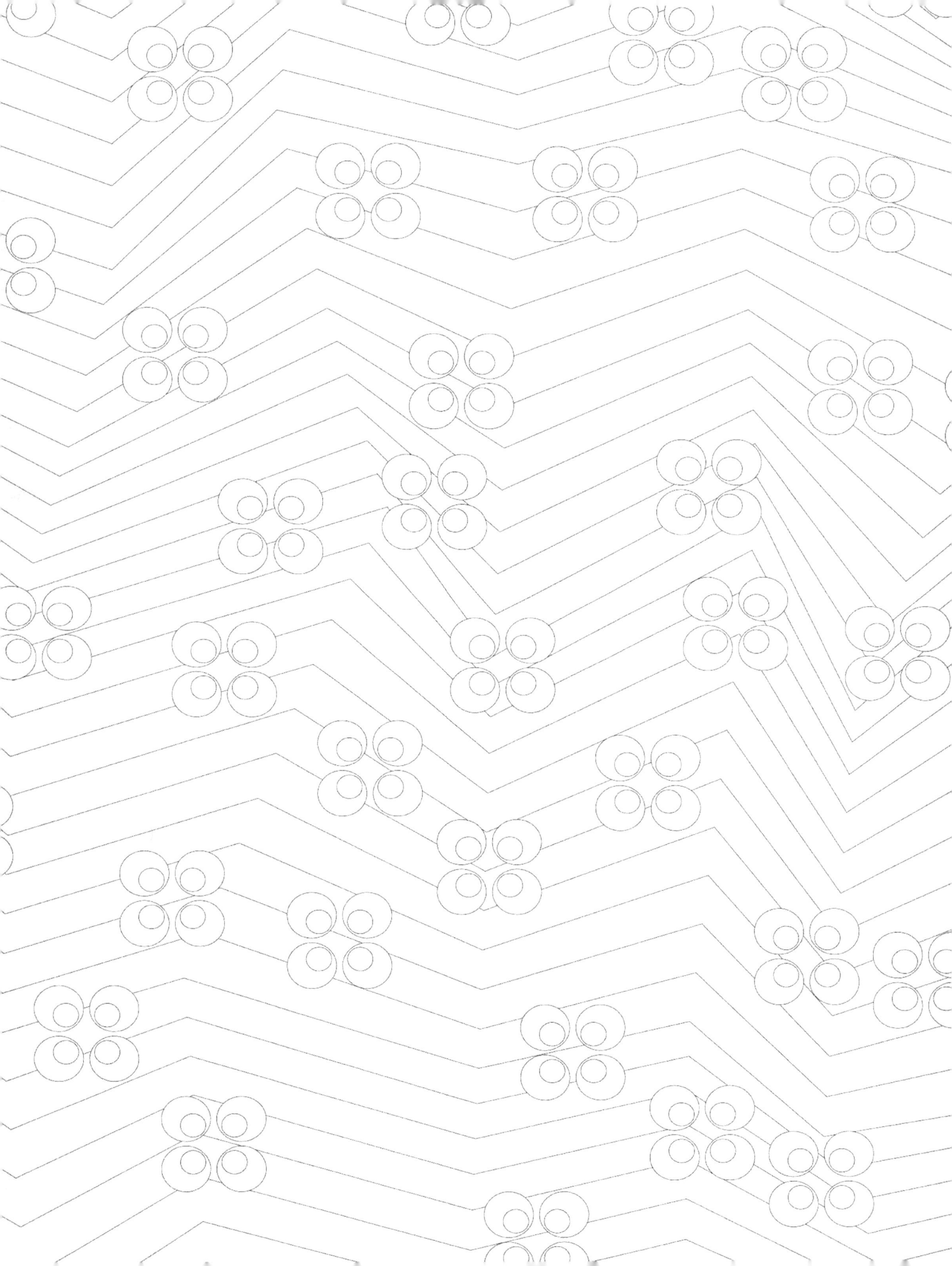

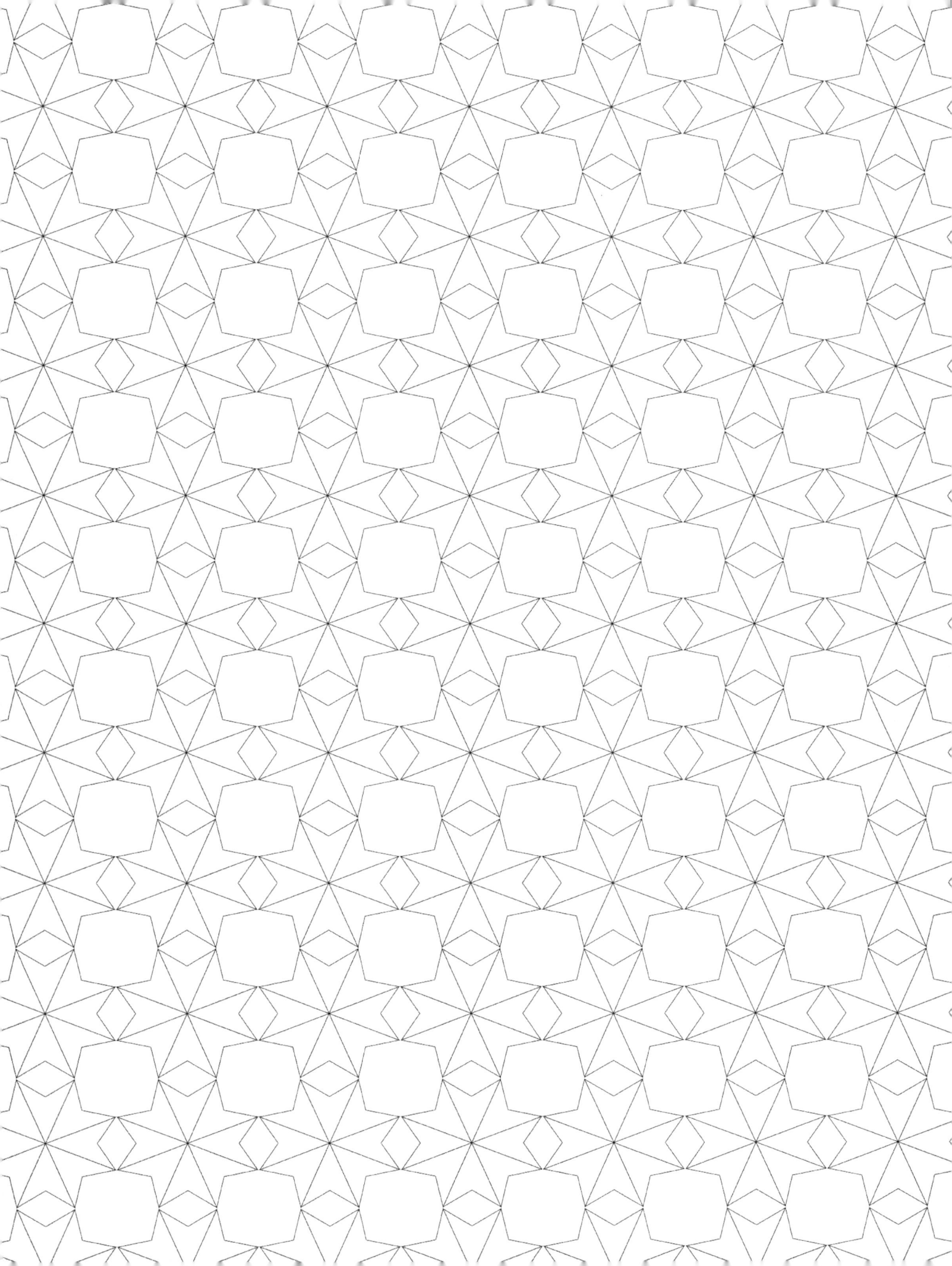

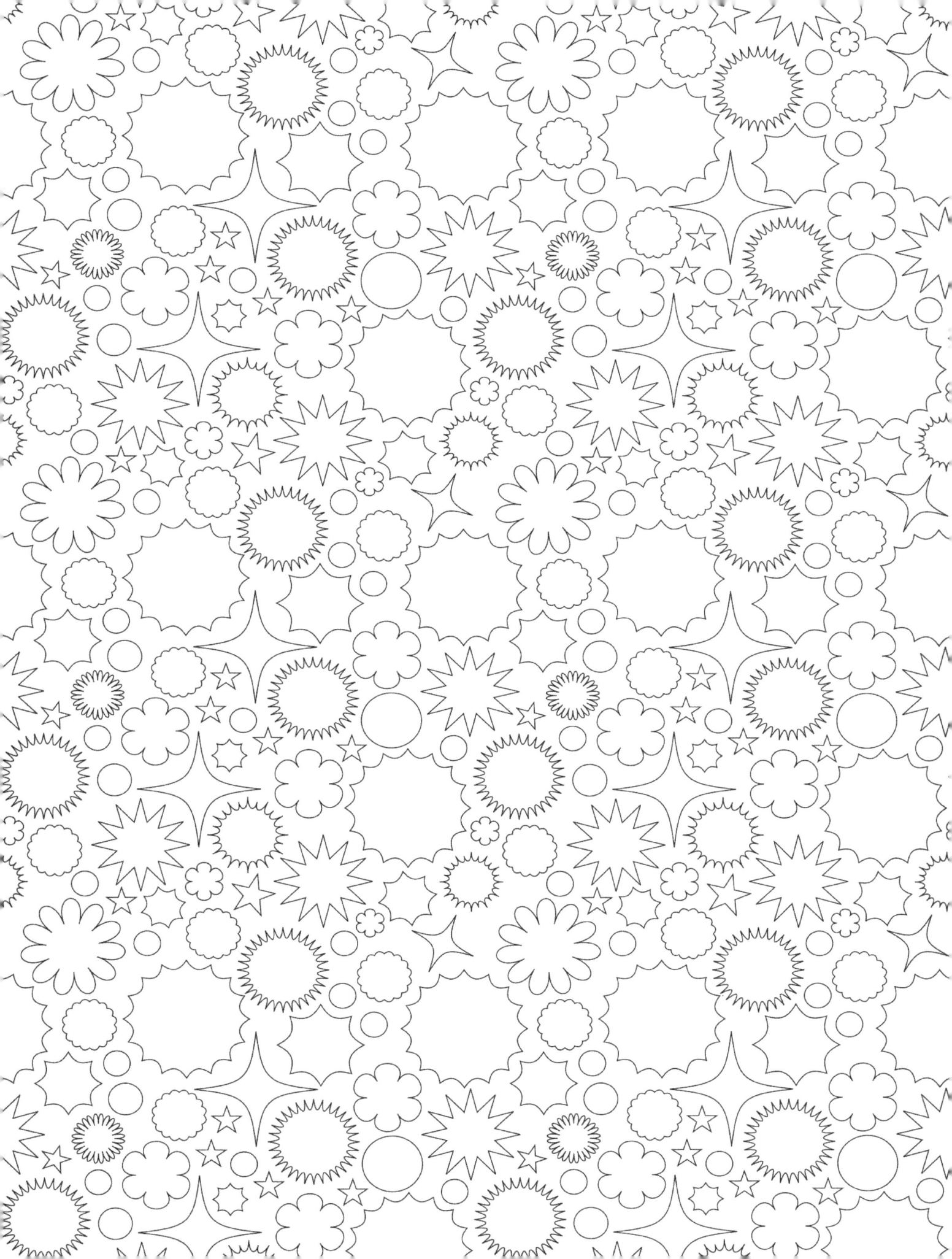

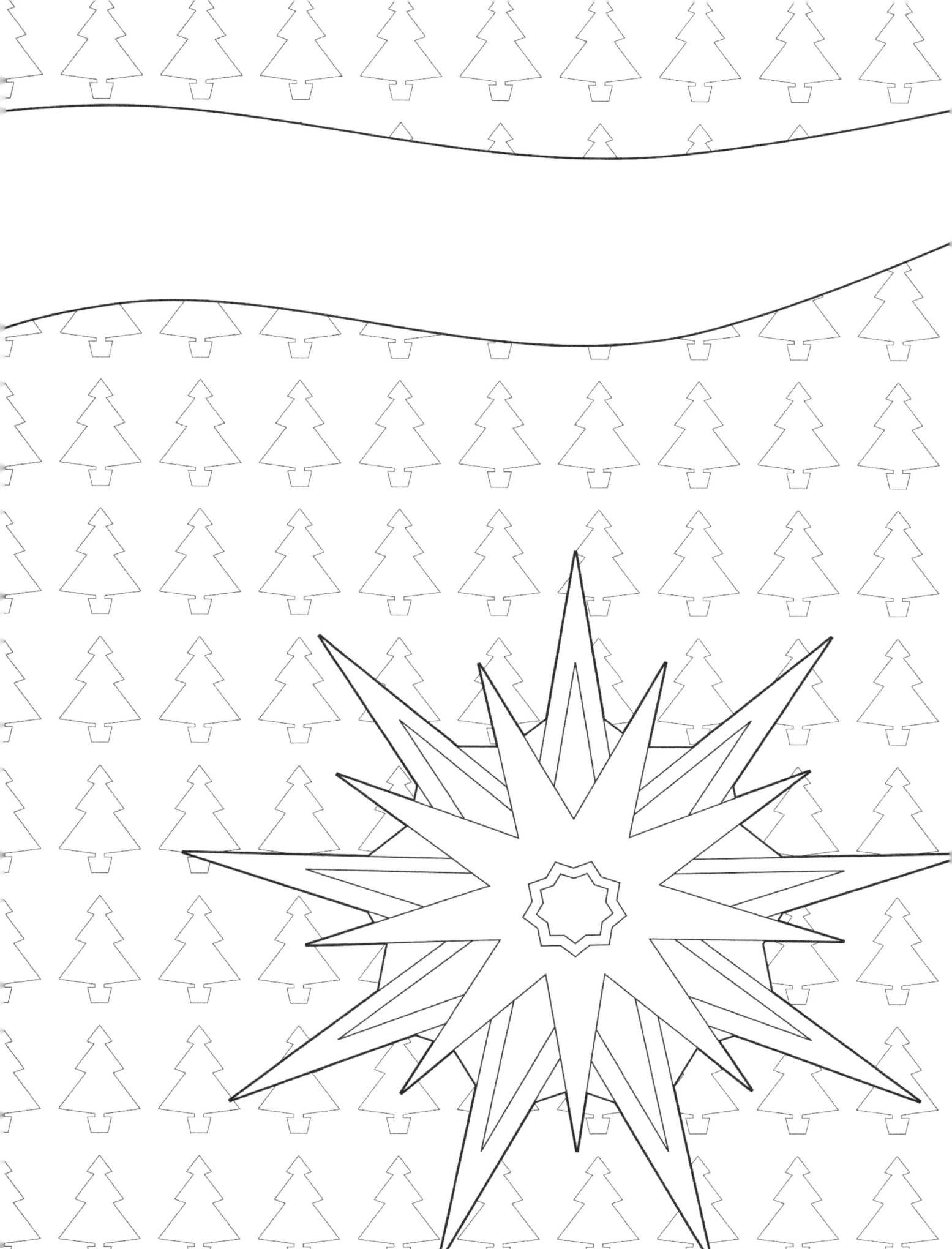

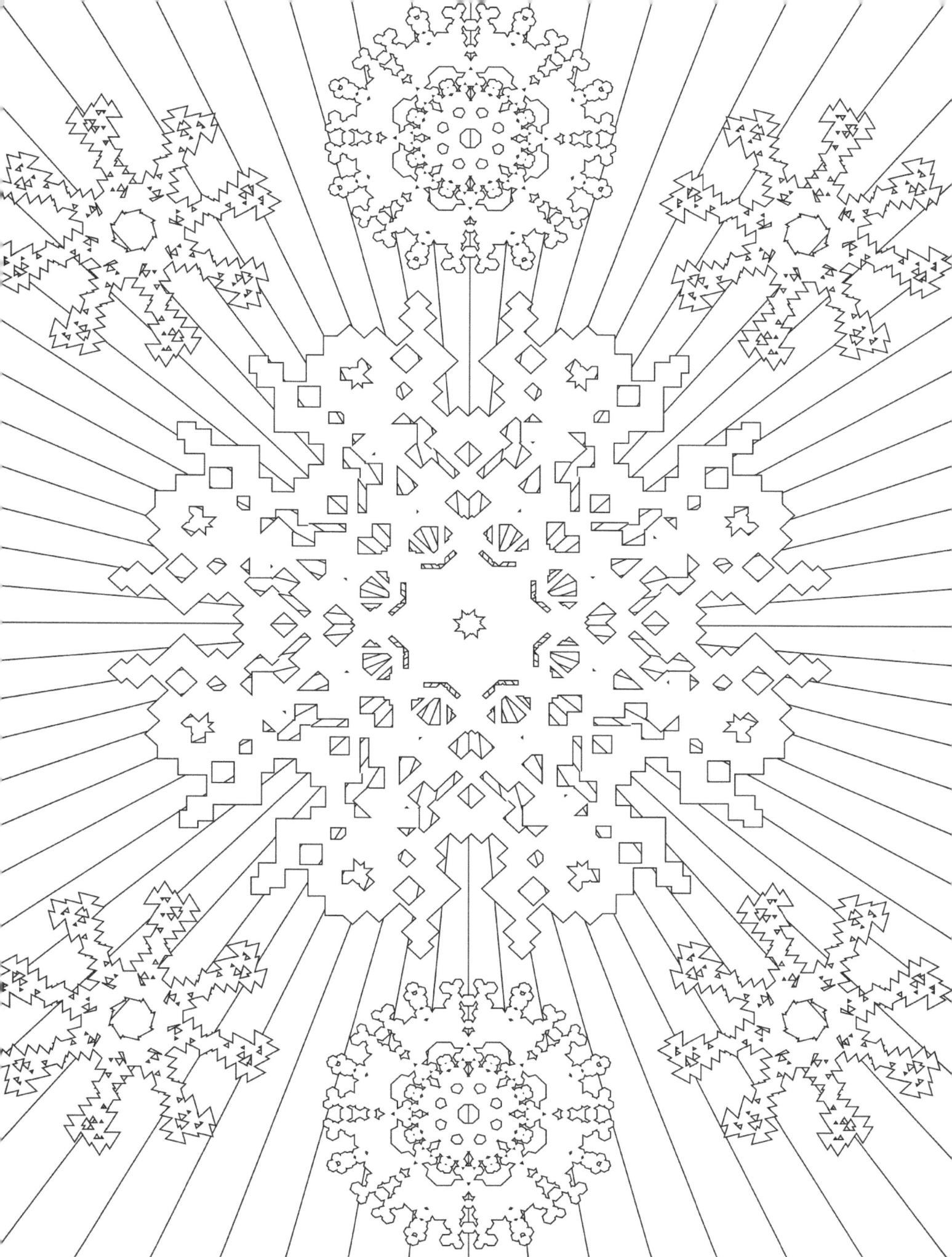

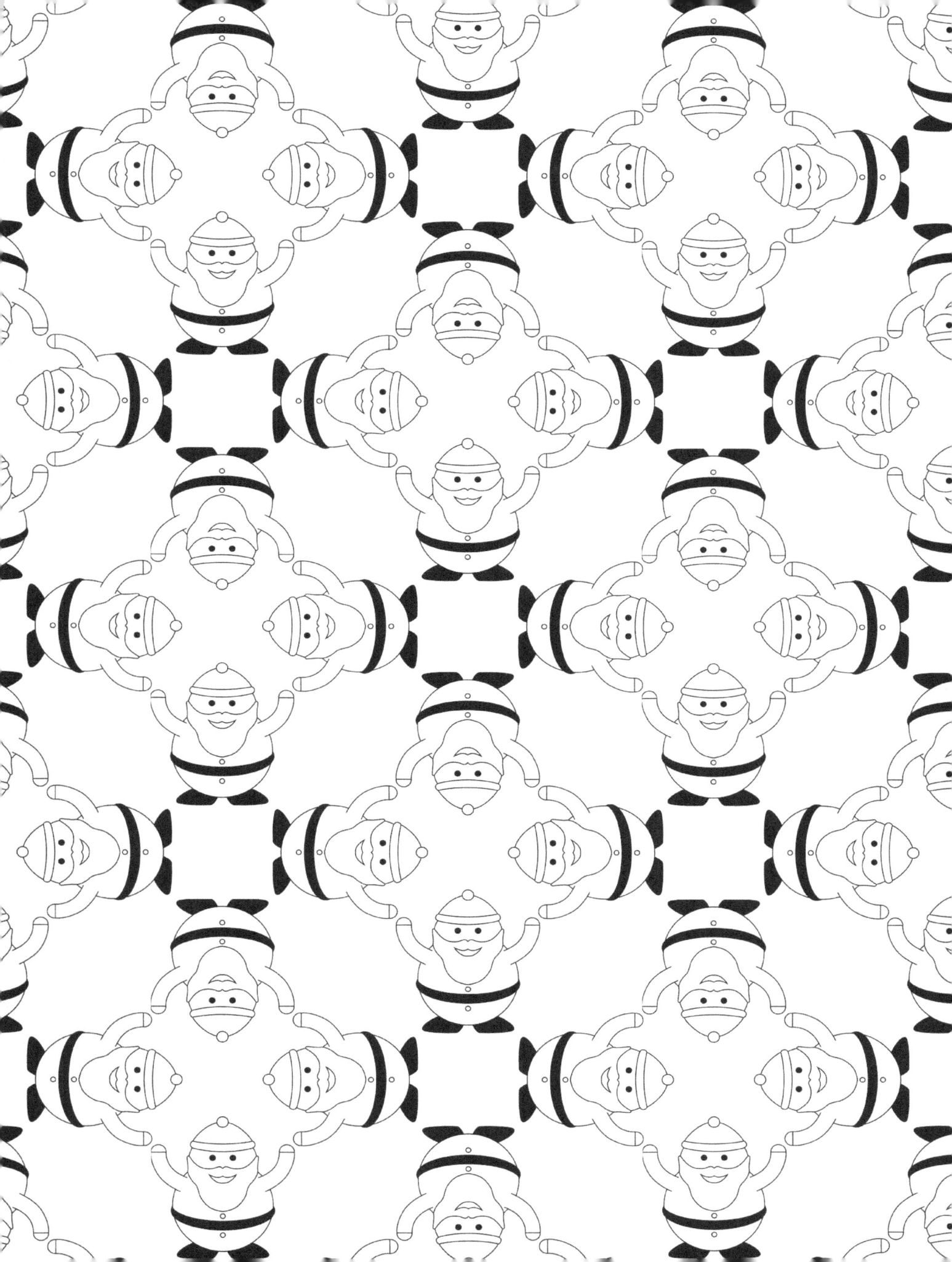

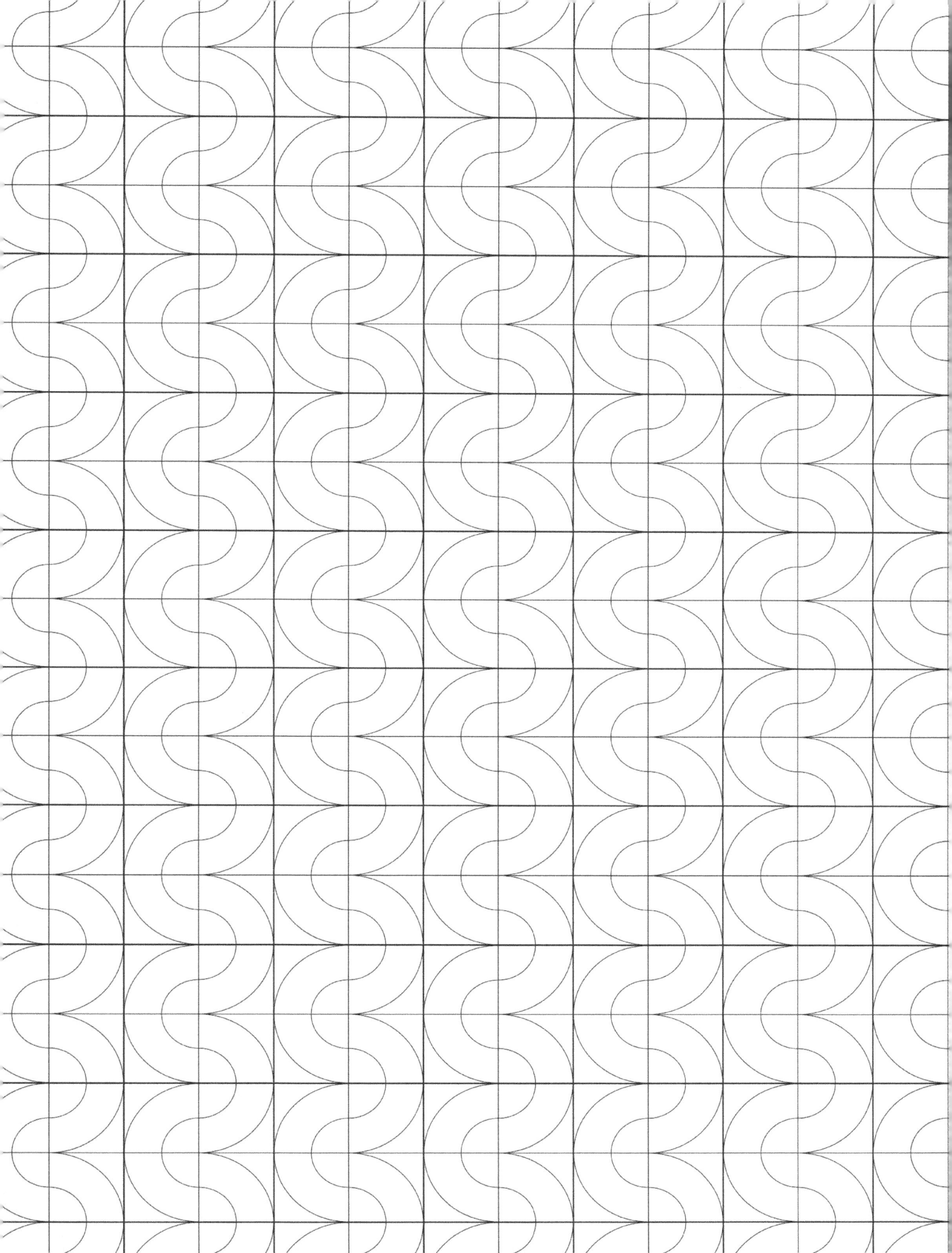

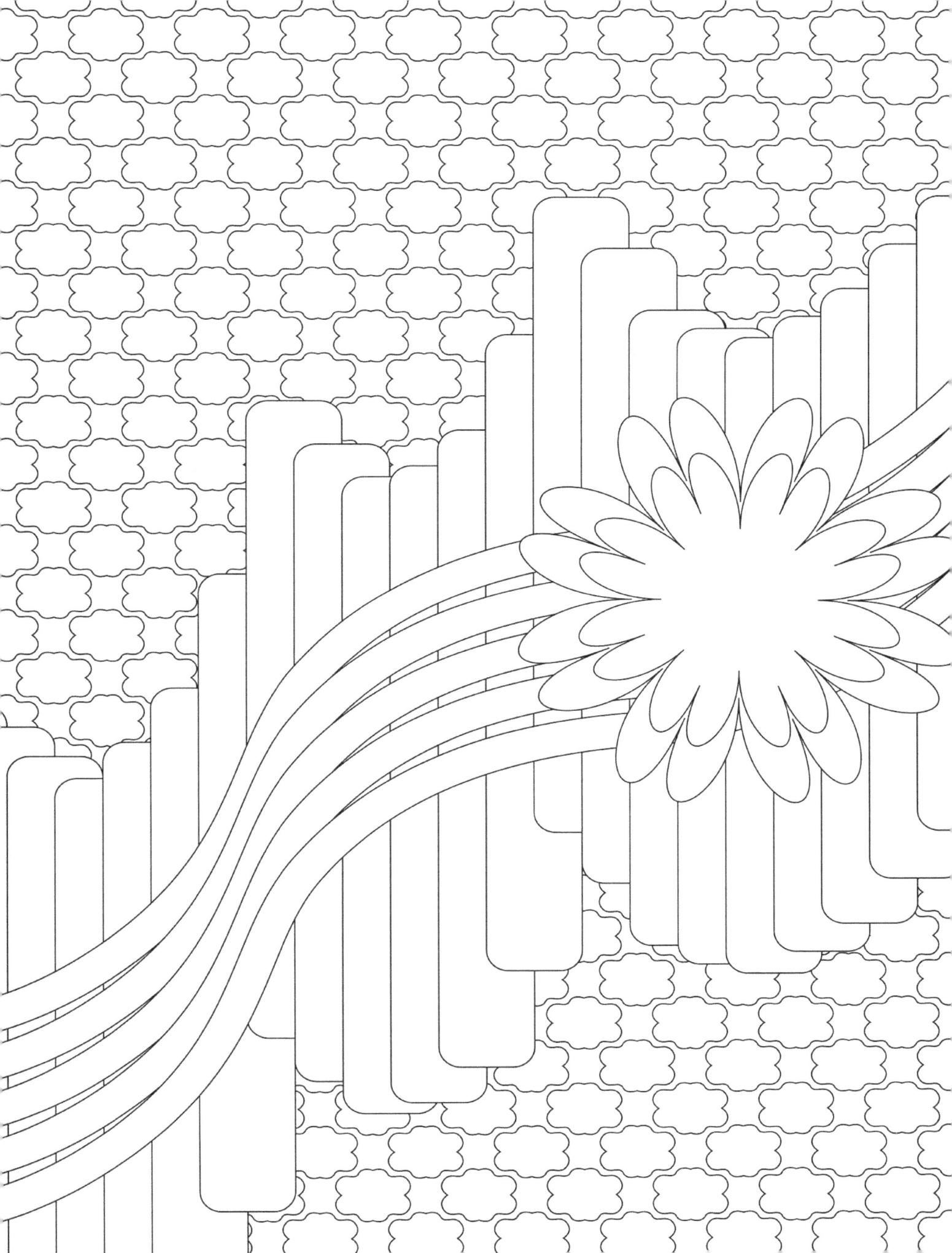

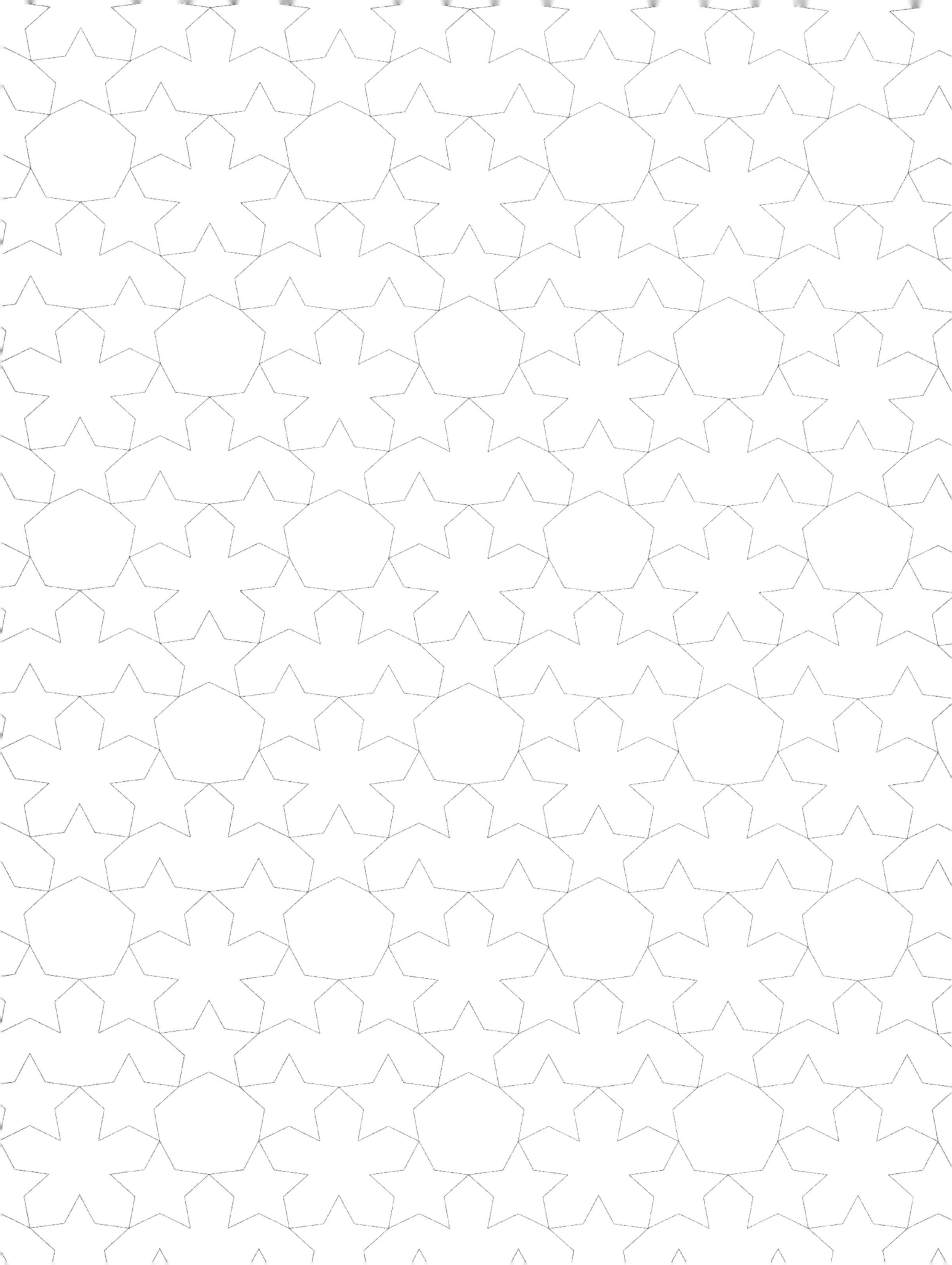

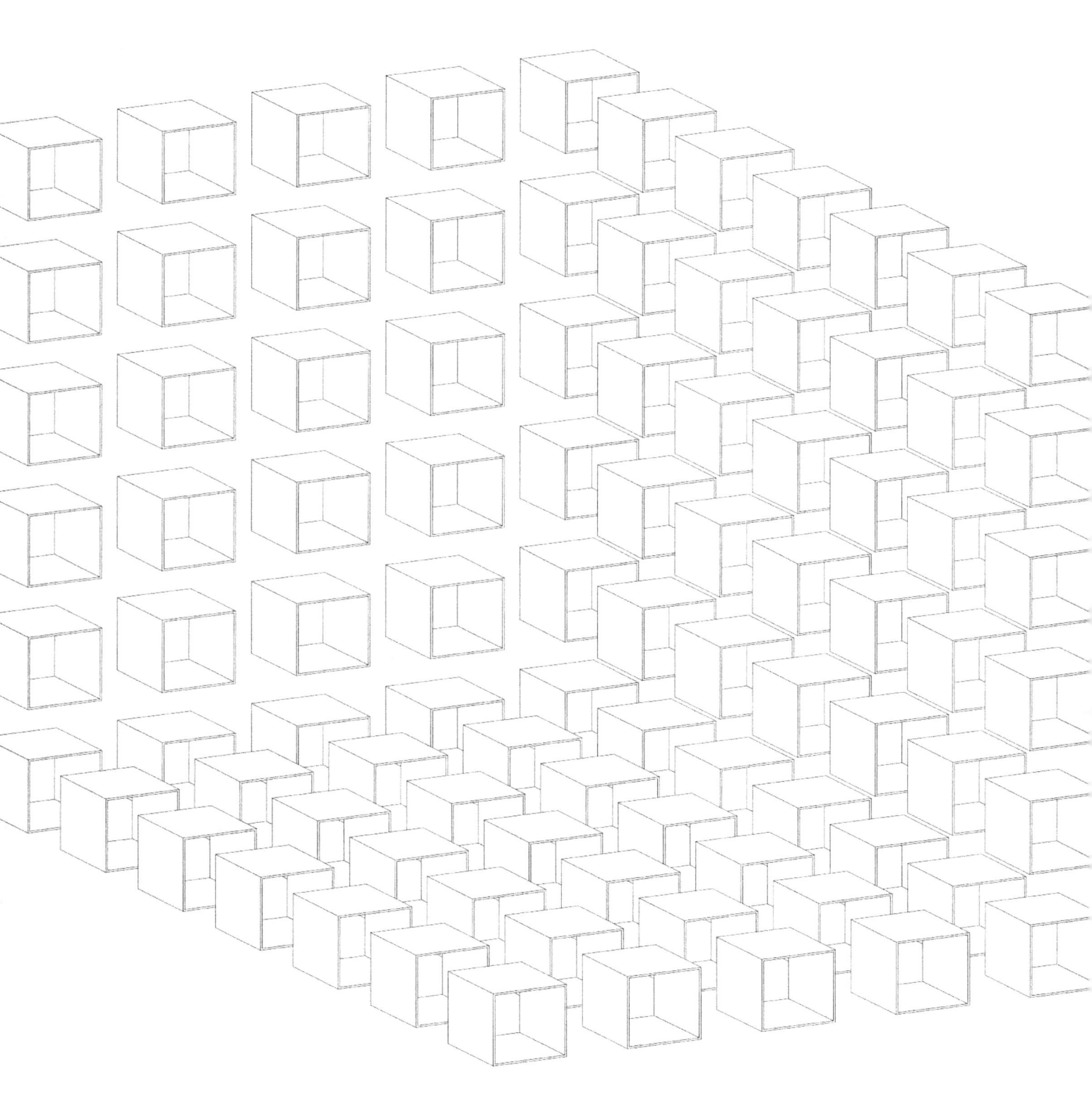

The End

www.ingramcontent.com/pod-product-compliance
Lightning Source LLC
Chambersburg PA
CBHW082031190526
45166CB00017B/2564